# FACE TO FACE WITH
# ELEPHANTS

## by Beverly and Dereck Joubert

NATIONAL GEOGRAPHIC
WASHINGTON, D.C.

# FACE TO FACE

**S**he came out at us like a rocket! She was hot, angry, and very large—a full-grown elephant with a look in her eye that showed she meant business. I suspected there were going to be a few bruises, some tears, a little blood—all of them ours.

My wife, Beverly, and I were looking for elephants. Photographing wildlife can lead you into some scary places. We were in a wild area in Botswana, far from civilization. When we heard splashing noises at a nearby river, we walked down to it, hoping to find

*Large, gray, and in a bad mood. When this elephant came at us out of nowhere, I knew we were going down!*

## THE SCOOP ON ELEPHANT POOP

Elephants are important to life in Africa, and so is their poop!

▬ Many trees have hard seeds. After elephants eat them and expel them, they are softened and ready to germinate.

▬ Flowery acacias and tall date palms grow along old elephant paths. Can you guess why?

▬ Baboons, birds, and insects raid the warm dung for seeds and other tasty treats. Yum!

▬ I use dung, too, to track elephants. I poke my finger into it. If it's still warm, that means the elephant is close by.

a herd of elephants. I spotted only three elephants, so we returned to our truck. We had removed the doors so we could get in and out silently. But this time, the springs groaned. Suddenly, the elephants at the river fell silent. They had heard us.

The forest brush exploded as the elephant cow charged at us wildly, head down, like a giant bulldozer. I started the engine, which will usually stop an elephant, but she didn't even hesitate. I was afraid she was going to ram the truck, so I slipped it out of gear. This way, it would roll easily when she hit it, and she wouldn't get hurt.

The truck shuddered as she rammed it. She was about an arm's length away—so close that I smelled her breath. Towering above us, she heaved with all her might, pushing us backward down the track.

Then I remembered that there were deep holes behind us. If she pushed us into one of them, we would tip over. I applied the brakes, and for the first time she couldn't move the truck. Now she was really mad. She lunged at the truck, smacking it hard and showering us with saliva. Chunks of ivory shot in at us like bullets when she chipped the tip of her tusk. This stopped her. She felt the chip with the tip of her

trunk, flapped her huge ears, and turned away.

We looked at each other and back at the elephant. Now we could see why she had attacked us. Under her chest was a cyst, a covered-over wound that can be painful. Elephants' thick skins heal fast, often trapping infections inside. Eventually, the infection can kill them. The wound looked as if it had been made by a bullet or spear. She had probably been attacked by poachers.

As we watched her go, I silently apologized on behalf of whoever had done that to her. We forgave her for coming face to face with us in such a rage. 🐘

*▲ Herds are often made up of individuals of different sizes. With binoculars, we scan them and check the various ages. You can see which years were good for breeding by counting the animals of each size.*

MEET

# THE ELEPHANT

I don't like being charged by an elephant. It ruins the trust that we spend so much time trying to establish. We try to be invisible, going about our work in the hope that they will ignore us, giving us time to understand them.

Elephants are wild and difficult to tame. They've got attitude, and I like that. At the same time, they are the gentle giants of Africa.

They care for each other in amazing ways. We once saw a baby elephant trapped in mud.

A very large male, like this one, can be terrifying, but some old males in their 60s are very calm. They spend their days munching on the soft river grasses in peace.

9

The whole herd worked together to dig him out, lift him up, and carve a ramp so he could climb free.

In an area with many poachers, we have seen elephants whose trunks had been cut off by traps, or snares. They survive only because others in the herd tear down branches and feed them.

They are also very social. It's fascinating to sit near them, just listening. There is a constant rumble, soft and very comforting. Everyone used to think these sounds were just indigestion. But thanks to scientist Katy Payne, we now know the elephants

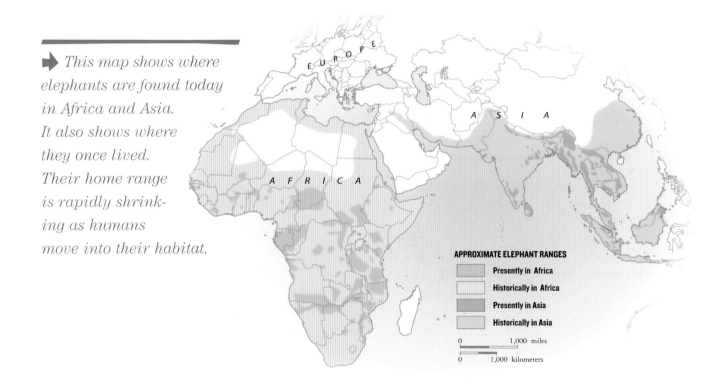

➡ *This map shows where elephants are found today in Africa and Asia. It also shows where they once lived. Their home range is rapidly shrinking as humans move into their habitat.*

**APPROXIMATE ELEPHANT RANGES**

Presently in Africa
Historically in Africa
Presently in Asia
Historically in Asia

0          1,000 miles
0        1,000 kilometers

are communicating. In addition to the sounds we can hear, they make low-frequency sounds that we can't hear. Payne used giant speakers and recorded hundreds of hours of elephant calls. When she replayed them for us, elephants drinking peacefully nearby swung around and fanned their ears to listen!

You cannot look into an elephant's eyes and not feel that there is a deep intelligence there, something ancient and thoughtful.

*This massive bull elephant, a symbol of Africa, stands like a giant on the plains. Elephants once roamed the continent from sea to sea.*

11

LIFE

# AS AN ELEPHANT

*An elephant herd is made up of members of an extended family. This closely bonded group consists of the adult females and their offspring. The average herd in Botswana has 8–15 individuals.*

The elephant's birth: It starts with a long drop to earth into a crumpled-up heap. The newborn looks like a miniature elephant in oversize skin, with feet that don't quite match or fit. Elephant babies may be funny looking, but the whole herd celebrates the birth. There is a lot of trumpeting and wailing. Everyone comes to see the little bundle of wrinkles, usually sniffing it with their trunks, probably to see if it is a boy or a girl.

The little one puts up with all this prodding and

jostling, but all it really wants to do is figure out where the milk is. That milk is in an udder between the front legs of its mom.

Pretty soon the baby is running (stumbling, really) alongside its mother. The herd takes giant steps. For each step an adult takes, the baby has to take 10 or 12 steps just to keep up. It looks exhausting!

Shortly after, the real fun starts. Baby elephants soon realize they can bully everyone else on the savanna and in the forests. They chase everything from small cattle egrets to big buffalo, and all creatures in between. Young elephants stay near their mothers for several years.

Between 12 and 15 years of age, the young females start attracting males and are able to mate. Around this time, they take on the role of *allomother,* or babysitter, helping to look after an older female's babies. Perhaps this is training for when they have babies of their own.

For mating to succeed, both male and female have to be ready. The male's period of readiness is called *musth.* If mating is successful, the female will give birth to a single calf 22 months later.

The leader, or matriarch, guards her family by gathering them behind her at any sign of danger. She fans out her ears to make herself look even larger than she is and scares off the attacker.

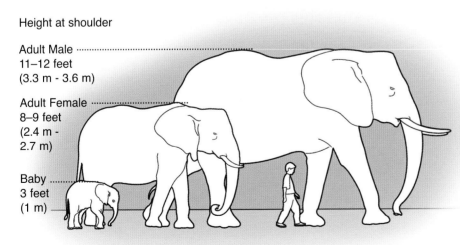

Height at shoulder

Adult Male
11–12 feet
(3.3 m - 3.6 m)

Adult Female
8–9 feet
(2.4 m - 2.7 m)

Baby
3 feet
(1 m)

Compare the sizes of elephants to a three-and-a-half-foot-tall child. A mature elephant bull is up to 12 feet (3.6 m) tall at the shoulder. Females are much smaller, up to 9 feet (2.7 m) tall. A baby that can walk under its mother's belly without ducking is less than a year old.

⬆ *Trunks up! We often see elephants suddenly stop and all sniff the air. They seem to be sensing the locations of other elephants or any strangers.*

Young males begin to drift a little farther from the herd as they get older. Usually this lagging behind ends with grumpy rumbles when they realize that no one stops and waits for them. But eventually the young bulls do leave the herd. With elephants, this is a gradual, gentle process. No one forces them away.

The young males join groups of mature bull elephants, old guys who lumber through the

Calves born around the same time, like these cousins, often grow quite close.

## ELEPHANTS HAVE A LOT TO SAY

Elephants have vocal cords in their throats and a special pouch beneath their tongues. They use these to communicate.

━━ By studying elephant behavior together with recordings of their calls, scientists have figured out the meaning of about 50 calls.

━━ Some elephant talk is at too low a frequency for us to hear, but elephants also make loud trumpet calls you can hear a mile away!

━━ You may not be able to hear them, but if you are quiet, you may be able to *feel* them talking. It's as if something is vibrating in your chest.

forest from waterhole to waterhole, smashing down trees to feed on and fearing nothing (except humans). This connection between young bulls and older bulls is vital. If young bulls grow up without the supervision of the older bulls, they get aggressive and nasty. In several instances, gangs of young "orphan" males in wildlife parks attacked and killed buffalo and rhino. It gave conservation managers a headache trying to figure out a way to control them. Finally, the managers introduced a few old bull elephants. Within a short time, the bulls took control, slapped the young males into shape, and formed a well-behaved herd.

The heads of extended elephant families are called matriarchs. Matriarchs are mature females who lead rich family groups. The great selflessness of these matriarchs is clear when there is the slightest hint of danger. We've seen

*If there is a true King of the Beasts, it must be the bull elephant. Everyone runs from him!*

elephants respond to threats all too often. The matriarch leader signals to her herd to gather around and behind her. She lifts her head up three feet (one meter) or more. Then the matriarch steps out, head held high, ears out wide, ready to take on the attackers. She dips forward and charges, with the entire herd behind her.

It's a strategy that scares off most things. Sadly, it is a terrible defense when humans are the threat.

⬆ *(left) Elephants seem to set aside time for play. On a sweltering day in Botswana (120°F; 49°C), swimming is the perfect way to chill out!*

⬆ *(right) Lions often stake out waterholes and the areas nearby, where herds are most desperate for water. They launch their attacks on stragglers and lone calves.*

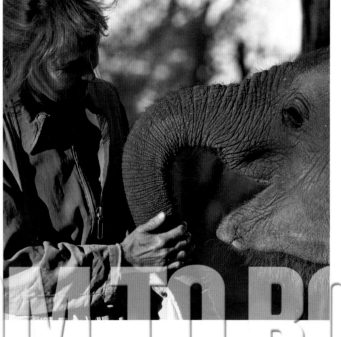

# ROOM TO ROAM

About 50 or 60 years ago, nearly two million elephants existed. Today, there are fewer than 500,000 left. Poachers seeking their long, gleaming ivory tusks are responsible for many of the deaths. Governments and even conservation groups have also killed elephants over the past few decades to control their numbers. When too many elephants live in a small area, the land is over-grazed and put under a lot of stress.

Some say the practice of controlling their numbers,

*It is now rare to find places in Africa that have enough space for large herds of elephants. In Botswana, however, they can roam over huge tracts of land in and around the Okavango Delta.*

called culling, is still needed. To do this, rangers challenge the herd and wait for the lead female to gather the members. Then they kill her. Without her, the herd is easy to destroy.

Most conservationists today have better ways to manage elephants. In Botswana there are about 100,000 elephants or more. (It's hard to get an

An elephant investigates the bones of a fallen friend. Sometimes elephants toss earth or branches over dead elephant bodies. It can't be scientifically proven, but we think they feel sad when they lose a friend or loved one.

accurate count because they move around.) But officials here don't cull the herds, nor should they. Many conservationists believe that the reserves and parks should be redesigned so that the elephants can travel along corridors, or safe roads, from one reserve to another. For example, in Angola, reserves have few elephants, so linking the reserves will ease the pressure on overcrowded areas elsewhere.

Some research suggests that elephants are clever enough to understand when there are too many of them and start adjusting their own breeding rates. I am not sure whether this is true, but ongoing research should tell us.

Lions are another threat to elephants. It is sad to see a lion kill an elephant, but it is nature's way. In Botswana, where we live, it seems to be happening more often. This is probably because the elephant population there is high, and when it comes to hunting, lions take advantage of any opportunity. Still, lions take just a fraction of the elephants.

Elephants sometimes cause problems for farmers, who don't like having their crops raided. In a single night, one elephant can wipe out enough corn to feed a human family for a whole year. Instead of

*An elephant known locally as Abu. He is a wonderful character and a giant in the world of giants.*

reacting violently, some people started growing chili plants, which are hot and spicy, around their other crops. Sure enough, elephants stayed away.

Photographic safaris (ecotourism) can help bring money to local people. This helps them see a real benefit from elephants. When the elephants are "paying" for schools and clinics, people will be more inclined to protect them and respect their corridors.

So the future for elephants could be very good, but they need space. By respecting these gentle giants and protecting the great open spaces they need, we help the Earth and enrich our own lives, too.

We once showed a film we did on elephants to the president of Botswana. Afterward, he held Beverly's hand and said, "Why can't we be more like elephants?" The words often ring in my mind. Yes, I wish we could be more like elephants too. It will help us share the future together.

## HOW YOU CAN HELP

■■ Don't buy or use ivory. Ivory belongs to elephants. Most people are shocked to discover that someone has to kill an elephant to create an ivory bracelet. You can gently let people know that an elephant had to die to provide that piece of ivory or trinket.

■■ Write to your representatives in Congress, asking them to strengthen the bans on trading in ivory. Let's not buy and sell products from dead wildlife!

■■ Refuse to go to circuses and shows that use trained elephants. Even if the trainers

*◄ Twins are rare. They occur less than once in a hundred elephant births, and seeing them is a real treat. One elephant baby is a lot of work for its mother, so I doubt twins are much of a treat for her! She will have to eat constantly for years to provide enough milk for them.*

aren't cruel, these animals are usually not allowed to live as they should, in groups, or with lots of room to move around outdoors.

■■ Spend some time in the company of elephants, even in a zoo, and just "be" with them. You may find that spending time with these gentle giants makes you feel better. It works for me! I realize that we are not alone as intelligent beings on this planet. I feel more whole, more connected to the world.

■■ The World Wildlife Fund and the African Wildlife Foundation are just two of the groups that support elephant research and make life better for wild elephants. Find out about their work at www.worldwildlife.org and www.afw.org. Maybe your family would like to contribute to these groups.

■■ Read all you can about elephants. Tell your friends and family about all you've learned. Knowledge starts with a small seed being planted.

## IT'S YOUR TURN

Would you like to see and photograph elephants yourself? You can start by visiting a wildlife park, or a zoo. Try to find one where the elephants are not separated into pens but are allowed to live as a group and spend most of their time outdoors.

*⬇ The trunk, weird as it is, evolved as a combination of the nose and the top lip.*

**1** Make a list of the kinds of things you would like to show. It could be the ways they use their trunks to eat and explore their world. Or how mothers and babies interact—a large zoo may have a mother and baby in residence. Or how elephants enjoy playing in a pool or even splashing water around in a tub.

**2** Get out your camera and notebook! Remember that elephants are sensitive creatures. Never try to get their attention by waving or throwing things, making loud noises, or acting wild. Never take a flash picture right in an animal's face. Stand quietly and observe. You will learn a lot without even trying. Use your notebook to write about what you see. Sometimes signs tell you the names, ages, and background of the elephants.

**3** National Geographic has a video game called "Afrika" that we helped with. It's a cool way to go on a virtual safari!

**4** In Africa, there are many opportunities to see elephants living wild and free. If you are lucky enough to visit, Botswana and Kenya are the best places to see elephants. In Selinda Reserve, Botswana, there are around 9,000 elephants. They stream down to the river at midday. What a sight! In Kenya, Amboseli National Reserve is great. We saw massive elephants at a lodge near there.

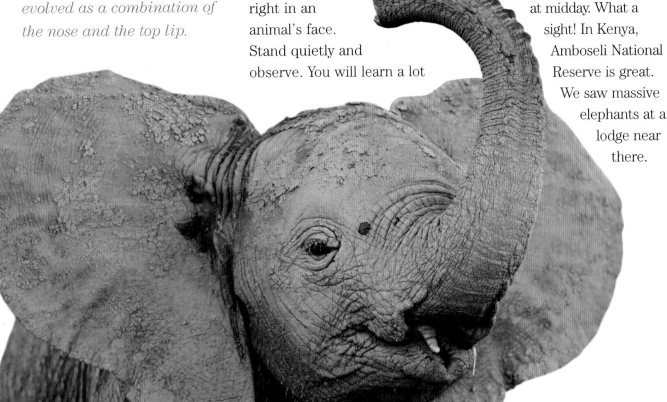

FACTS
AT A
GLANCE

■ **Scientific Name**
*Loxodonta africana*

■ **Common Names** Elephant (English); Tlou (Setswana); Nglovo (Zulu); and in East Africa, Tembo (Swahili).

■ **Population**
Elephants move around and are hard to count. The International Union for Conservation and Natural Resources estimates there are less than 500,000 of

◄ *The Asian elephant,* Elephas maximus *(top), has small ears, a large head, and thin tusks. It is only distantly related to the African elephant,* Loxodonta africana *(bottom). African elephants have large ears—shaped like Africa!—and carry their heads level with their shoulders.*

them left in Africa. It classifies African elephants as "vulnerable." That means wild elephants are at risk of dying out.

■ **Size**
African elephants are the largest species of land animal. Adult males are up to 12 feet (3.6 m) tall at the shoulder. Females are up to 9 feet (2.7 m) tall. Adult males weigh up to 16,535 lbs (7,500 kg), females up to 7,125 lbs (3,232 kg).

■ **Lifespan**
In the wild, elephants live 60 to 70 years. In zoos, elephants can live up to 80 years.

■ **Special Features**
The elephant's trunk, with more than 50,000 muscles along its length, is an amazingly useful part of its body. First, of course, it is a nose, used for breathing and for smelling things. The sensitive tip can also curl like fingers to pick up objects as small as toothpicks. But the trunk is also strong enough to uproot a tree. Elephants use their trunks to

stroke each other, smack opponents, and throw objects around. They even use them as snorkels, holding the tips in the air while they swim underwater.

Adult elephants of both sexes grow tusks, which developed from specialized teeth. They use their tusks to defend themselves, but also to dig up plants, salt, and minerals that they eat, or to dig holes in the sand for water. Elephants favor a right or left tusk, just as you favor your right or left hand.

Elephants' feet look big, but they actually walk on the tips of their toes. Most of the foot acts as a soft cushion. A whole herd of elephants can travel very quietly when they want to.

Elephants' skin is tough and thick, but they don't have much hair to shield them from the sun. That's one reason they roll in mud. It acts as a sunscreen and protects their skin.

### Habitat

In East and southern Africa, elephants live on the grasslands, or savannas. Forest elephants live in West and central Africa. In Namibia, elephants live in the desert. These tall elephants survive on very little water. In the wetlands area in Botswana, they virtually live in water, bathing every day. Elephants are protected in many parks and reserves throughout Africa.

### Food

Grass, fruit, palm nuts, tree bark and stems, leaves—lots of them. In fact, elephants eat around 400 pounds (200 kg) of plant material a day. They drink up to 60 gallons (225 liters) of water. They eat no meat at all.

### Reproduction

Mating takes place over a week when both male and female are ready. Female pregnancy, or gestation, lasts a long time— 22 months. She nurtures and suckles the calf for two more years before mating again. This means that elephants can breed every four years at most. Young elephants stay near their mothers for several years. Females remain with the same family group all their lives.

### Social Habits

Wild elephants live in groups of related individuals, led by a mature female. Young males leave the herd, joining other bulls or living alone. Elephants usually follow regular routes from one grazing area to another, or move with the seasons to find the best feeding grounds. They travel and feed both night and day. Elephants communicate across distances with low-frequency rumbling calls. They seem to have very good memories for places, other elephants, and people. They also keep track of where other elephants are by scenting them on the wind, or checking out piles of dung.

### Biggest Threats

Except for lions, elephants are not hunted by most predators. Growing human presence on wild lands in Africa threatens elephants when people want land for crops. Poachers who hunt elephants for ivory have caused the greatest drop in the elephant population.

# GLOSSARY

**Allomother:** a female elephant who cares for another elephant's offspring.

**Bull:** a male elephant.

**Calf:** a baby elephant up to around 12 years old.

**Charge:** the forward rush of an attacking elephant.

**Cow:** a female elephant.

**Ivory:** the material that animals' teeth are made of. Elephant tusks are especially sought after.

**Low-frequency sound:** sound below the range that most humans can detect. Many animals can hear low-frequency or very high-frequency sounds that we can't hear.

**Matriarch:** the female head of a family or extended family.

**Musth:** a state of readiness for mating in male elephants. Musth bulls can be a little cranky and tend to charge more often than males not in this phase.

**Poaching:** the illegal killing of a protected animal.

**Tusks:** incisor teeth that grow curving out of the upper lips of elephants. Tusks can be ten feet long.

# FIND OUT MORE

## Books & Articles

Douglas-Hamilton, Iain and Oria. *Among the Elephants.* New York, NY: Penguin, 1978.

Joubert, Dereck and Beverly. *African Diaries.* Washington, D.C.: National Geographic, 2000.

Joubert, Dereck and Beverly. *Whispers: The Story of a Baby Elephant.* New York, NY: Hyperion Press, 1999.

Moss, Cynthia, and Colbeck, Martyn. *Echo of the Elephants.* New York, NY: William Morrow, 1993.

Poole, Joyce. *Coming of Age with Elephants.* New York, NY: Hyperion Press, 1996.

## Films

*Whispers: An Elephant's Tale.* Walt Disney, 2000.

*Reflections on Elephants,* by Dereck and Beverly Joubert, National Geographic Television, 2000.

## Web Sites

www.wildlifeconservationfilms.com

www.awf.org/content/wildlife/detail/elephant

www.iucn.org

www.sandiegozoo.org/animalbytes/t-elephant.html

# INDEX

# RESEARCH & PHOTOGRAPHIC NOTES

I've already told you how to start understanding elephants, and I think this is what it takes, really, getting to know your subject. We've known great photographers and filmmakers, but it's the people who have empathy for elephants that achieve the best images. What we like to do is get down low, much lower than the elephant's line of vision. We do this to accentuate the tremendous size of these animals. I love to see them up against the sky, rather than cluttered against the brush.

Beverly uses Canon cameras and a vehicle full of lenses. You wouldn't think you could use anything other than a wide angle lens really, given the size of these creatures!

I will always remember something I used to do as a kid with my brother, who is an artist. We took a picture of an elephant and cut it in half. He took a piece and so did I. We both had fairly good representations of the elephant. We cut our halves in half again. We could still see elephants. We cut again and again until we finally looked up at each other, realizing that we'd gone too far. But we had also done what Japanese artists are so good at, finding the most iconic picture, the very essence of that animal or image.

With this in mind, both Beverly and I compose our pictures as minimalistically as possible. This is a great discipline, to find the one part of an animal that represents the whole species. Play with framing just the one thing that *is* an elephant—no, not the dung!—but the tusk and maybe that wise old eye. Light that and compose for just that. It's haunting and tells a story at the same time. It is mysterious, but not so weird that you have to look at it for days to figure out what it is.

Africa, life—everything, really—is made up of small details. Many of them just symbolize the whole.          —DJ

FOR THE GIANTS THAT COME
BEFORE US: THE ELEPHANTS,
CYNTHIA MOSS, JOYCE POOLE,
IAIN DOUGLAS-HAMILTON, KATY
PAYNE, RICHARD LEAKEY ... ALL
AMBASSADORS AND WONDERFUL
FRIENDS OF ELEPHANTS. —DJ & BJ

*Acknowledgments*
Our first thank-you goes to an elephant
cow that charged and hit us hard one
night, upended us, and left us shaken but
alive. She changed our lives and made us
live one day at a time. We have been
inspired by some great elephant people:
Iain Douglas-Hamilton, whose book I was
reading when I first decided to work in
the bush; Joyce Poole; Cynthia Moss;
Katy Payne; the owners of Wilderness
Safaris, in whose reserve we live and
work; the President and people of
Botswana; the Ministry of Environment
and its Department of Wildlife and
National Parks for permitting us to do
our work. The National Geographic
Society has inspired us and so many others worldwide with its work. For years
the Society has supported our research,
photography, and filming, but only
recently have we become fully aware of
the extent of its efforts to inspire people
to care for the planet. Last, to the
elephants: Dear Sir/Madam, we are sorry
for what we humans have done to you.
—Dereck and Beverly Joubert

Back cover photograph by Jacques
Nortier (copyright Wildlife Films).

Book design by David M. Seager.
The body text of the book is set in
ITC Century. The display text is set
in Knockout and Party Noid.

*Published by the*
*National Geographic Society*

John M. Fahey, Jr., *President and*
*Chief Executive Officer*

Gilbert M. Grosvenor,
*Chairman of the Board*

Tim T. Kelly,
*President, Global Media Group*

Nina D. Hoffman, *Executive Vice*
*President; President, Book*
*Publishing Group*

*Staff for This Book*

Nancy Laties Feresten, *Vice President,*
*Editor-in-Chief of Children's Books*

Bea Jackson, *Design and Illustrations*
*Director, Children's Books*

Amy Shields, *Executive Editor*

Jennifer Emmett, Mary Beth Oelkers-
Keegan, *Project Editors*

David M. Seager, *Art Director*

Lori Epstein, *Illustrations Editor*

Jocelyn G. Lindsay, *Researcher*

Dianne Hosmer, *Indexer*

Carl Mehler, *Director of Maps*

Rebecca Baines, *Editorial Assistant*

Jennifer Thornton, *Managing Editor*

Grace Hill, *Associate Managing Editor*

R. Gary Colbert, *Production Director*

Lewis R. Bassford, *Production Manager*

Maryclare Tracy, Nicole Elliott,
*Manufacturing Managers*

Susan Borke, *Legal and Business Affairs*

*Front cover & pages 2–3:* Face to face
with an African elephant; *front flap:* An elephant calf; *back cover:* Dereck and Beverly
Joubert with one of Africa's gentle giants;
*page one:* A young elephant raises its trunk,
sniffing out danger.

Library of Congress
Cataloging-in-Publication Data

Joubert, Beverly.
 Face to face with elephants / by Beverly and
Dereck Joubert.
    p. cm.
 ISBN 978-1-4263-0325-8 (trade)—
 ISBN 978-1-4263-0326-5 (library)
 1. African elephant. 2. African elephant—
Pictorial works. I. Joubert, Dereck. II.
Title. QL737.P98J67 2008
599.67—dc22

2007041229